Edited by Helen Exley:
Grandmas and Grandpas (1975)
To Mum (1976)
To Dad (1976)
Happy families (1977)
What is a husband? (1977)
Cats (and other crazy cuddlies) (1978)
Dogs (and other funny furries) (1978)
Dear World (1978)
A Child's View of Happiness (1979)
A Child's View of Christmas (1980)
What is a baby? (1980)
Love, a Celebration (1981)
What it's like to be me (1981)

Picture research by Wendy Sacks

First published 1982 © Exley
Publications Ltd, 12 Ye Corner, Chalk
Hill, Watford, Herts, United Kingdom,
Second printing 1982

Typeset by T & R Filmsetters,
77 Salusbury Road, London NW6 6NH

Printed in Hungary by Kossuth
ISBN 0 905521 18 8

Illustration credits:
Art Directors Photo Library (pages 4,
37)
BBC Hulton Picture Library (page 35)
Barnabys Picture Library (pages 9, 31,
46/47, 48, 61)
M. A. Barnard (page 16)
Camera Press (page 22)
John D. Drysdale/Colorific! (front
cover, page 51)
John Doidge (page 6)
Elisabeth Photo Library (page 18)
Mary Evans Picture Library (pages 15,
35, 39, 41)
Richard Exley (pages 29, 52)
Keystone Press Agency (pages 21, 25)
Rex Features (pages 10, 13, 18, 55)
Tom Kennedy/Source Photographic
Archives (page 43)
Rob McKnight/Source Photographic
Archives (page 57)
Tony Stone Photolibrary – London
(pages 27, 33, 44, 59)
ZEFA (front cover)

The photographs in this book have been
supplied by photographic agencies
and photographers independently of
the text. The women are not
necessarily wives, and the
accompanying text does not
necessarily apply to the actual lives of
the people appearing in the
photographs.

WHAT IS A WIFE?

Edited by Helen Exley

Anne looked her best on the day we got married. That was about six stones ago.

J. E.

The morning after

On the wedding day, assuming there is one, the man should see his wife at her best. If she doesn't look too good then he should remember that from now on she will be going downhill.

Bernard J. Hockley

A wife is someone who very early in marriage gets taken off a pedestal and put on a budget.   *Anne Phillips*

A wife's way of life changes from billing and cooing to bills and queuing.   *D. D. Brown*

In the first year following the tying of the knot the couple will wake up to the reality of one another. Now, the successful businessman who has married a blonde barmaid from his golf club begins to wonder why he did it. The wife already knows – she engineered it carefully.   *Bernard J. Hockley*

I don't think that ever in history have women been led on to expect so much of marriage. The wedding list itself is no longer one of basic needs but a glittering dream of gadgets. The wedding has spiralled into fantasy. And however humble her flat the sound of ad men's voices is steady and insidious as the sea. With their white linen, cleaners that snuffle up dirt, dinners straight from the rajah's table, kids that are healthy, intelligent and winsome, husbands that are alive with charm and sex and reliability . . .
It is no wonder that the wife coping with her hideously spotted, chicken poxed youngest child while trying to unravel the pluperfect tense for her despairing eldest – hemmed in by ironing, damp walls and a husband having trouble with his transmission – wonders if she's been sold a pup.
Once she's got used to the reality she may find being a wife not at all bad. Just totally different to what she was led to expect.

Penelope Smith

Before I married, life was like a reasonably taxing game of chess. It never dawned on me that once you were married you switched straight away to a three-dimensional board.   *Edward B. Langley*

Wives are people who make their husbands take off their dirty shoes when they come in from the garden completely forgetting they used to say they worshipped the very ground he walked on.

Capt. A. R. Quigley

5

*A wife is a living
contradiction of the belief
that civilization is based
upon the division of
labour.*

Marian Quayle

Just a slave

Every wife has inside her the ghost of Carroll's Queen of Hearts. As she washes mud-plastered rugby shirts, wipes up talc, picks up tacks and hoovers up shavings, she roars inwardly, 'Off with his head!' It is a miracle of nature that there are not more headless husbands.
Pamela Brown

A wife is the person who does today what the rest of the family are always going to do tomorrow.
Marilyn Morris

My wife wore a radiant smile as she was ushered out of church after our son's wedding. When I asked her if she could remember what she had been thinking at that happy moment she said, 'Of course. Only half the shirts to iron!'
G. W. Sanders

All the women I know with immaculate houses are paying someone else to do the housework. I don't know what the moral is but wives who say a house isn't lived in unless it's a bit untidy quickly change their minds as soon as they can afford it.
Michael Herrick

Husbands do weightlifting in the secrecy of their bedrooms. Wives do theirs in the High Street.
Robin May

A pathological study should be done on the length of women's arms after thirty years of marriage. Surely bags of potatoes, tin cans and shoe repairs must have *some* effect?
Dee Waring

Husbands say 'Why don't you do one job at a time?' – or call you butterfly brained. No one asks them to answer the door bell, tend to the cat, calm the baby, watch the sauce, make a note about the leak in the sink, wipe up the spillage, chase out next door's dog and try to work out what her husband called out as he went out that morning – all at once. No wonder not many wives get down to writing epic novels.
Elizabeth J. Sands

Only a wife will write all the Christmas cards, buy all the presents, get in all the food and drink, do all the baking and then be asked why she doesn't enjoy Christmas.
Joy and John Edwards

My wife says that she is a slave. She says that if I paid her the wages that she earns looking after me, I'd be in debt for a hundred years. My wife says that she is the best money manager that I know. What's more, she says she must be an angel to put up with my scruffy ways. She told me that she doesn't know anyone who works so hard for so little reward, and that only *I* could burn holes in every decent shirt I possess and still expect them to be washed and ironed. Another thing she said is, that without her, I'd be a nobody, with nothing to my name.
You know, I think I believe my wife.
J. D. Bryant

Unromantic moments

She's the one who *knows* that the gleam in your eye is really just your contact lenses. *S. J. G. Caldwell*

She runs her finger through my hair like she did when we were courting even though I've only three left. *A. Bourne*

The women in the other beds in the maternity ward were in bowers of Interflora blossoms. My husband arrived late with a bunch of gladioli. 'Got 'em half price! He was selling them off!' *Victoria Hurrell*

A wife is someone who lets me keep my fishing maggots in the fridge during warm weather. *P. B. Carman*

To become a wife is to become the holder of secrets. Only their wives know the black comedy of a bank manager with mumps; the whimpering self-pity of a long-distance lorry driver with a heavy cold; the dismal spectacle of the star of the local Rep. in faded striped pyjamas snoring his way through influenza; the deflated figure of the hero of the local football team moaning with indigestion. Their underlings, rivals, fans and drinking cronies wouldn't know them. For dignity's sake they mustn't know them. Their wives put on kettles, fill hot-water bottles, dissolve aspirins – and restore them at last, good as new, to an unsuspecting outside world. *Pamela Brown*

A wife is someone who, in the middle of love-making asks: 'Did you turn off the gas?' *P. Cronin*

A wife is the apparition which climbs into bed in winter wearing three jumpers, two nightdresses, a pair of tights, bedsocks and a dressing-gown. *M. G. Plaxton*

A wife in love with Shelley or John Donne is likely to find her husband a little inadequate. It is easier to love the safely dead than the untidily living. *Tony Scott*

The only happy wife is one who accepts that a great part of love is ridiculous. *Meg Anderson*

The times when a woman plans divorce is when her husband calls her ... 'Dear, the cat's been sick'.

Emma Palmer

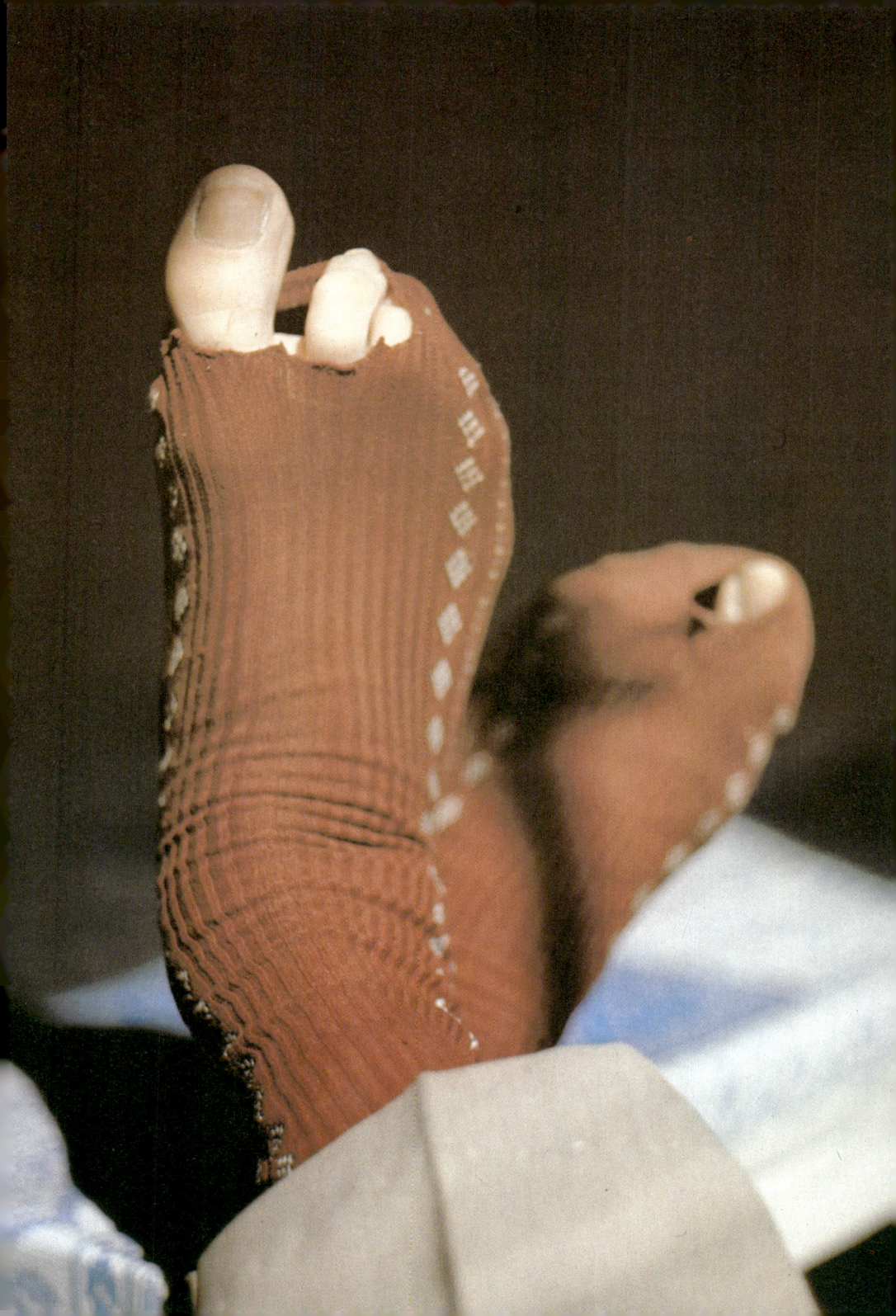

Useful gadgets to have around

A wife is a washing machine on two legs.   *Brian White*

A wife is a one-woman laundry.   *Jon Atkinson*

They're the only ones who can make lump free beds.   *M. Sanders*

I can pack just as well as she can. But she doesn't forget my tooth-brush.   *Peter Simons*

Wives are regarded as having a built in ability to deal with sick, blood and worse. Husbands have queasy stomachs.   *P. Brown*

A wife is a hot-water bottle with arms and legs.   *David Peet*

A wife is a system of levers for getting me out of bed in the morning.
Andrew P. Staite

She's the only one who knows exactly how and where to scratch your back.   *Gerald Parkinson*

They're magic. Who else can mend the television with a kick?
J. Bates

*A wife was the name
given to the first
labour-saving device
invented by man.*

Colin Quayle

11

Under every good man . . .

A wife is expected to run around fetching things whenever a husband deigns to do a job in the house. 'Where's the ladder gone? Have you moved my screwdriver? I'll do it if you can find me the pliers.' A woman just gets on with the job. What would happen if she refused to get dinner and stood around looking helpless, saying, 'Where's the saucepan?'
Angela Lansbury

Slowly realization dawns that married bliss has more to do with washing socks than the romantic state you had dreamed about. Trudging in from work, loaded with two heavy shopping bags you say to yourself, 'Am I a wife or a camel?' and stagger into the kitchen to prepare *his* evening meal, averting your eyes from the inviting chair by the fireside. His key turns in the door – enter the man of your dreams. 'Haven't you got my tea ready yet? I *am* tired!' says he cheerfully, sinking into the chair and switching on the television. It is one final straw when this poor tired man, having downed his tea shoots out to the rugby match leaving *you* to do all the washing-up.
Marian Cleworth

A wife is somebody who wouldn't be able to get a union job carting heavy loads around yet is expected to carry heavy toddlers, wet washing, bags of potatoes and frozen food.
Michelle Barnes

A wife will stand in queues all her life; usually at the back.
B. J. Davies

A wife gets to read The Observer when she is parcelling potato peel.
Wendy Chapman

Wife to husband: 'What is a wife?' Husband to wife: 'Don't ask me conundrums. Go and see if dinner's ready.'
Angela Sharot

An expensive asset

A wife always thinks of only three things: MONEY MONEY MONEY.
H. Haines

A wife is the cause of that fallacy that two can live cheaper than one.
Will Hazell

A wife with money is a shopkeeper's dream and a wife without money just uses her husband's credit card.
M. G. Plaxton

They do so much work that most people think they're a good investment. Husbands know better; they see the phone bills.
William Jackson

A wife is someone who buys a hat for 20p at a jumble sale, then spends £20 on a dress to go with it.
John Tate

A wife is a person who is sent to buy anti-freeze and comes back with a fur coat.
H. Haines

A wife is someone who spends slightly faster than a husband earns.
K. Shriver

A wife believes in sharing everything – as long as it belongs to her husband.
M. G. Plaxton

Wife, plaintively, 'I can't remember the last time when we went out for a good meal.'
Husband, reading bank statement, 'Good. Just keep on not remembering.'
A. Sharot

Only a wife can say she is always saving me money by buying something that says £10 off — and then buying something else with the £10 she has saved.

John Edwards

Photograph by M. A. Barnard

16

The competition

It's mostly when I see a lovely, new racy looking model in the street that I'm tempted to consider changing my old one for a new one. Some of them are such lovely jobs with smooth bodywork, beautifully tailored upholstery, and they move so well.
Mind you, mine was a beauty when I acquired her some years ago. In fact she's not bad now and quite economical to run, but then I've always looked after her as I said I would.
Another thing, one gets so attached, you get to know their good and not so good points, when to nurse them along a bit and when to put your foot down to get the best performance.
And I think; suppose I did get a new one, I might be unlucky, get a bad one and have nothing but trouble. I don't think they always make them as good as they used to, do you?

Ray Capper

To find out
what a wife is,
go back to Mum
for a couple of
days.
You'll soon
realise what
the missing
ingredient is.

M. Stratford

Love, cherish and Oh! Boy!

A wife is someone who is always around. Very round here, very round there and very round you know where.   *Alan Connor*

She turns me on when she comes to bed in a nightie but she turns me on more when she comes to bed without a nightie.   *A. Smith*

Reach out in the night.
Slip an arm
Round a soft tum.
Grip a hand,
Squeeze.
Pull near, close, warm.
With a desperate longing.

Two bodies,
Joined.
The thousand and first time,
The same power, the same joy.
Urgent.   *Richard Alan*

A good wife enshrines all the qualities and appeal of your best friend's mistress. She should, additionally, offer much easier access, be more practical and, paramount, know none of your friends.
     Paul Berry

The first year was in the 'altogether' followed by twenty years of assorted lace frillies which in turn was followed by silk pyjamas – now after forty years and a pair of rheumaticky legs it's a long flannelette nightie topped off with a bed jacket on cold nights. But, for all that, she can still turn me on. That is the hallmark of a real wife.   *D. W. Bull*

Wives fall into three main categories:
1) Those who love, honour, and cherish.
2) Those who love, honour, and obey.
3) Those who love, cherish, and Oh Boy!   *Capt. A. R. Quigley*

Making it all worthwhile

A wife is the only person in the world you feel as at home with as your own self. *David Skinner*

A wife is the warmth I feel when I return home from work. She is the atmosphere of my family and the tender kisses of a mother. *Bill Dennison*

A wife is someone whose absence makes the house feel strange – as though you'd wandered into another dimension. *Brian Hill*

I make the living and she makes it worthwhile. *E. Smith*

A wife is the person a house waits for, uneasy till she's safely back. *Patrick C. Hodson*

A Chinese proverb tells us that 'A hundred men may make an encampment, but it takes a woman to make a home'. *A. J. Bucknell*

You grow up together, stay forever, sharing, meeting all kinds of trouble, thinking of the jobs to be done.
Through laughter and tears which come and go in everybody's life, a wife is the first to get things moving again as if they had never happened, flowers on the table, and a nice evening meal. *N. Thornton*

A wife is the lovely person, who fills our house and home with love. *J. Hickson*

Home Sweet Home could never have been written by a bachelor. *W. A. Page*

Without a wife there would be no children's laughter, no world, no anything.

J. W. Harvey

For love

Nothing gives a man the desire to live and to live it more abundantly, than a beautiful woman. *E. E. Laycock*

She's the person you can spend twenty four hours a day with, sit in silence with, argue with, and always feel a bond with – that nobody can come between. *W. A. Armstrong*

When you are young you mean to do such a lot of things. Falling in love and getting married is a sort of extra. And then the years go by and nothing works out quite as you'd planned and you find the only thing that lasts is what you feel for each other. It changes. It alters all the time – but maybe that's the reason it survives. *P. Brown*

My neighbour is built like a Russian heroine of industry. Her husband looks like a weasel with a moustache. Everyone's idea of the music-hall comic couple. Yet they live a life of most marvellous contentment, each deeply involved in their individual careers, yet the best of friends and companions. They have a hugely successful daughter, built on the same plan as her mother, whom they both regard with awe. And when you talk to the wife, at the mention of her husband, her great craggy face flowers into affection. 'He's a lovely bloke, my Charlie. A *lovely* bloke.'
Good wives come in all sorts of packaging. *Frank G. Armstrong*

If you think of a tree too hard, it turns before your eyes into a huge structure of cells and chemical reactions, then to atoms, electrons, a total illusion. It's the same with love, with marriage. Theorize about it, dissect it, examine it under a microscope and it turns to a phenomenon of race continuance and social structures, psychological need and economic necessity. Which it is – and it isn't. For I'm not a statistic – I'm a husband. And I love this bundle of electrons which is my wife. And that fills all the empty universe. *Neil Kemp*

There is no applause in marriage. No one applauds a flowering tree.
Harold Philips

They must be something. Why else would all these millions of hulking great men go down on their knees to get only one each?

G. Marks

23

The world of families

I suppose before I married I judged everything and everyone by my standards – and even when there were difficulties, I had largely only myself to consider. Once you are married you become involved not only in your husband's life but in living as a whole. It's no longer a matter of causes, but people. Even watching the news becomes harder – they are somehow all *your* husband, *your* kids.

Ruth Newton

Before I married life was like a diet of meringues and beefburgers, fizzy drinks and ice cream. Now I'm a wife it's bread and butter and beef stew, jam roly poly and tea. Somehow more solid. Much more satisfying. I feel much more calm – it's as if my whole nature was putting on a bit of useful weight.

Just as long as I don't let it turn into a dull, immobile stolidity!

Joanne Adamson

When you become a wife you begin to learn not only how to live with one other unique individual – but with the world as a whole. I think before I married I saw everyone else as background to my own life – now I see that they are each the centre of their own universes – and just as 'real' as me.

Heather Jones

How can anyone say what a wife is? A thousand women, a thousand different definitions. Each looks for something different, each brings to their marriage what they are and makes of it what she can. Each marriage must endure a different set of sorrows, know different joys. Each has a different breaking point that may or may not ever be reached. For some, when trust goes, they can no longer stay a wife; for some it is debt, or drunkenness, for some it is a long belittling.

Yet marriages endure and wives still love when many would turn away. Some seem to have the capacity for devotion that blots out any recognition of evil in the husband. Some endure insult, betrayal, physical violence and criminality with blind devotion. Duty, religion, habit, love, an inability to stand alone, a need to be needed – they can keep a marriage afloat. Some wives build so firm a delusion of security, that their husbands need do nothing – and the children are safe. Some, choosing between two evils, gather up their children and run.

And those who are patient and endure find a world that sickness and failure, loss and mistake cannot injure. These wives grow wiser with the years, their love, their own capacity for love, deeper and more subtle in its joys and its perceptions. So that all they are and all their husbands are, live in their secret safely, a world of which their neighbours know nothing and which their friends only suspect.

Pamela Brown

When I was single I used to
debate world problems and
read the newspapers with a
certain detached interest.
Now I'm married I don't see
'problems' any more — just
husbands and wives and kids.

June Smith

We two are one

Marriage is a paradox. You married to become closer – and find that for all the poetry and symbolism you are as apart as ever; Siamese twins sharing the same blood stream, yet still each his own secret self. Somehow in this separated proximity you must learn to co-operate – or die. Probably for the first time in your life, you realise fully that another person is as real, as alive, as much the centre of their own universe, as you are yourself. You must never forget it. You share a single cell – and yet you are distant as two stars.

You must learn to talk to each other. Not as you did before marriage, in the clichés of ordinary speech, but as clearly as it is possible for human creatures to do. Your lives depend upon it. You had thought that once the door was closed upon you, it would be warm, safe. But you find, locked in together, nothing is free of the other's hands. Tasks, habits, routines are fingered and changed, criticized and questioned. You are alone, yet never alone.

And the masks are gone. When you were first in love the darker, sillier, more peculiar aspects of life could be pushed into a drawer. You could in turn misinterpret signs of weakness, cruelty, stupidity, laziness. Now the failings are all in the open. Somehow, if you are to endure, you must face the fact that you are married not to a prince, a hero, a kind companion, a man of intelligence and virtue – but to a human being who cuts his toenails in the living room; is afflicted with heavy catarrhal colds, snores, belches and forgets to pay the gas bill. Heaven only knows what he has discovered about you.

Romance must go at last – and something better or worse take its place. You must learn to love each other as fallible, creating human beings.

And the paradox returns – for locked together in one chrysalis, two human creatures, altering with every moment under each other's needs – a great change can come at long last – and a new creature lurches out of the chaos to spread its wings in the sun. And that is when you can call it a marriage.   *Pamela Brown*

She is simply my alter ego. How can one define her? How can one separate a soul from a body, a song from a bird?

In marriage there should be sharing. It is a partnership. If the sexes insist on splitting themselves into *his* and *hers*; or try to tear themselves apart for the sake of self, there can be no bliss, or true meaning to marriage.

No! A wife is not another person. A wife is unity. And if a wife only sees her own image, then I suspect she is more liberated, than loved. To be as one is not submission, or subservience. It is simply a twin-quality, summed up in one splendid old-fashioned word – devotion.   *John Richards*

A wife is a spiky, complex creature brought into conjunction with another spiky, complex creature. For the rest of their lives they will be working out how to fit into the small world of marriage without damaging each other.

Jimmy Meacher

I'd do anything for you

A wife is someone who washes down and paints the ceiling while I hold the ladder, and wears my dressing gown for half an hour before I get up in order that I may put it on warm. She is someone who, when I had back trouble, slept on the board with me on the floor, and puts up with me when, going for romantic strolls in the country, brings a bag of horse manure back for my tomatoes. *A. Bourne*

I nursed my husband, who was house-bound for six years, he lost his sight and as a result lost his interest in life, then his memory went, and he lost control of his organs. I washed him, bathed him, dressed him, loved him. Last year, he passed on, eighty years of age, now I am all alone. I have an easy conscience, knowing I remembered the vows I made and I find comfort with my memories of joy and sorrow. I would gladly do it all again for the man who was 'Mate o' Mine'. *E. Watts*

A wife to me is someone you want to get home to. During my six years RAF service I travelled a distance of 18,040 miles by rail, 5000 miles by cycle, 1,400 miles by car, 500 miles by bus, and fifty miles on foot, a grand total of 24,990 miles just to be able to spend a few hours with her on my weekly days off duty.
During these six years of weekly travel home, I spent a total of twenty-seven days twelve hours waiting on railway platforms for connections. Many men would have done the same, but not unless they had the perfect wife waiting for them at the end of their journey – I DID. *L. K. Newling*

A wife is someone who stays up to keep me company to watch a late night horror film on telly, knowing she'll spend much of the time with her fingers in her ears and her head pressed against me as they frighten her sick. *Jim Jerred*

What I have got is a Human Robot who has cared for me, a chronically sick invalidity pensioner, and reared a family of seven without ever a moan or a groan. She should have finished as five of our children are married. But not her. She goes on caring for our grandchildren, without any reward. God bless her. *J. L. Jones*

A wife is the person who can keep her nerve and get a 'Heart Ambulance' out on my first heart attack.
A wife is the partner who gives up smoking so as to encourage her husband to do so and says she is giving it up because she is a nurse.
A wife is the person who visits the Intensive Care Unit and holds your hand and tries to look cheerful although she is crying inside because you are very seriously ill and may not survive.
A wife is the person whom you love with all your repaired heart and realise that without her you would be lost and all the surgeon's skill would have been in vain. *D. N. Beck*

Today I was reading the part 'in sickness' in *What is a Husband?* and after crying my heart out, I couldn't help thinking what my father would write about my mother. Enclosed is what I am sure he would write if he could. He has multiple sclerosis and has lost his power of speech.

'A wife is someone who I dreamed that I would like to say 'thank-you' to. Thank you for loving me all these years, for washing me, feeding me, changing me. I would dearly love to share the same bed again, to touch you, to tell you all the things I have wanted to tell you all these years. You don't have a life of your own anymore, you are the missing parts of me. You cannot go out and you worry about me, but please don't. I am just content that you have stayed by me, and will stay until the end.'   *Dianne Raybauld (for Tom Cooper)*

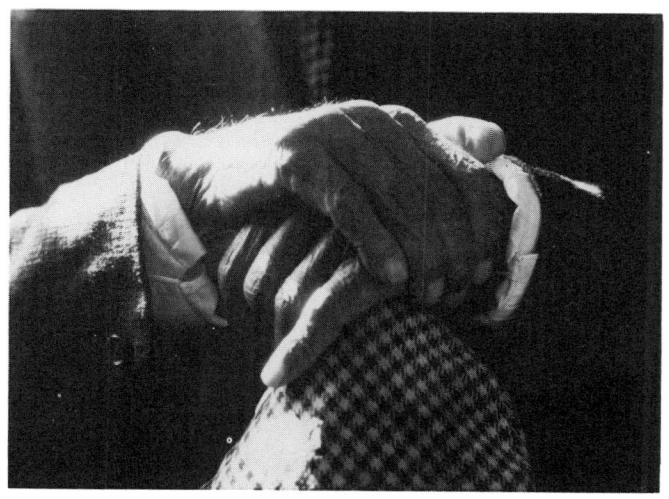

She is the one, (when times were hard, and food was scarce) who said 'I have eaten before you came home'. How can you repay loyalty, affection, motherliness? If I live a thousand years I shall never know.

B. Taylor

A kaleidoscope of wives

If the people she lives with can't sew on buttons, don't know how to use the washing machine, can't find where the loo rolls are stored, then she *must* be a wife. *W. Brand*

A wife shares the house, the bank account and the bed. A wife keeps house, her own Deposit account and most of the blankets.
P. Marchant

A wife is a secret 'Cheesy Whotsit' eater. *P. Wainwright*

As a nineteenth century writer put it, a wife has a whim of iron.
David Smith

A wife is someone who, before marriage, dreamt of Aisle, Altar, Hymn... once married she dreams, 'I'll alter him.' *T. Robins*

A good wife must have thousands of faults – and at least one more than her husband. *Mark Burley*

A wife is a cuddly millstone. *I. Neill*

A wife is someone who after I've gone to bed writes on my lunch banana 'I love you Juicy Lucy', then I miss seeing it and a female at work says 'Hello what's this'. *Philip A. Wright*

A wife is a person to whom you give up half your food to get the other half cooked. *R. M. Denholm*

A wife is a born diplomat who lets you have her way. *J. Gaff*

What is a wife?
Don't ask me.
Ask my wife.

Albert Lansbury

A wife is a sound driver. When parking she listens for the crunch then stops!

L. Millington

More wives!

When I married my wife I thought she was an angel – and I still think so. I've three reasons for this. First, she's always up in the air; second, she has never got anything to wear, and lastly, she is always harping on about something. *D. Bridger*

Have you noticed how few saints had wives? *P. Carlton*

Wives have perfect taste. That's why they choose husbands. *Jack Parker*

What is a wife? An optimist married to a greater one. *A. Marshall*

Men always refer to women as 'the wife'. Women don't refer to men as 'the husband'. Do men mean 'the wife' like 'the cat', or 'the wife' like 'the queen'? I've never liked to ask. *Netta Lansbury*

A wife is someone you take to entertain your mother while you read the newspaper. *B. Fenton*

A wife falls in love with the perfect man, then spends the rest of her life trying to change him. *D. D. Brown*

A wife is someone who cuts the 'Page Three Girl' out of my newspaper before I get down to breakfast. *J. W. J.*

A wife is a woman who warns a husband against women. *K. S. Dobie*

Men and children have 'flu in bed. Wives have it at the kitchen sink. *Catherine Murray*

A wife has different chromosomes which make her suffer from tidyitis. *William Straine*

A wife is someone who wants to keep all abandoned cats and dogs. You'd like to say no but you remember when she took you in. *Matthew Frost*

A wife is civilisation's best invention, a living paradox, a contradiction in curves, a spare ribful of surprises.

David Peet

Know your place, woman

Husbands are allowed to stray from the straight and narrow. Not wives.

Think of the words that describe a wife who strays: nymphomaniac, promiscuous, slut, whore, cheap, tart, floozy, mistress and a dozen similar words.

What do people call a male tart? Or don't they make that judgement?

Can you think of a list of words which apply only to the errant man?
B. Thoms

The difference between a wife and her husband's secretary is that the one is unpopular for reminding him of things to be done while the other is unpopular for failing to do so. *R. Phipps*

When a husband rigs himself out in torn, worn, stained and shapeless clothing, he calls it 'dressing casual'. If his wife tried the same thing, he'd divorce her for 'letting herself go'. *Patsy Thomas*

A wife is someone to shout at when the car won't start, and kiss goodbye when it does. *D. D. Brown*

When I have an accident it's carelessness. When my husband has an accident it's the other bloke's fault. *Jacky Franklin*

Men can never quite believe a woman, much less a wife, doesn't know how to drive, or the workings of a car. Once my husband misjudged the turn into our gate and put a wheel over the edge of the very sharp stream embankment. He leaped out to look, yelling 'Put the hand brake on.' We had to get a crane to get it out. I can't help thinking it wasn't entirely my fault. *Anne Short*

The first week I was married my husband told me it was an old rugby tradition that wives cleaned their husbands' boots. I told him that I regretted bitterly the decline in so many fine old traditions but there, one couldn't halt the tide of change.

He never really liked me after that. *Paula Simpson*

A wife is a woman who is listed in the phone book under somebody else's name. *Angela Lansbury*

There is nothing that rattles a husband more than an incompetent wife other than a competent one.

S. Pringle

The ducking stool (ABOVE), the famous remedy for curing shrews, was used throughout the Middle Ages. It was last used in 1745.

The stocks (BELOW) were an alternative.

The modern role

What a wife is expected to be is dictated by her time in history, her geographical placing. In the past we more or less knew what the job was, what to expect. Love was an unexpected bonus. We learned to work in the fields, run an estate, raise a child or bully housemaids. We knew our expectations, we expected to lose our children, to die young, to suffer a good deal.

But at least we wore one bonnet. Now, with all the labour-saving devices and health care and legal protection, we simply don't know *what* the job is or, often, who we are. The Saxon wife wasn't expected to serve *Cordon Bleu* meals or wrestle with gas bills. As they faced plague and hunger, dirt and cold, a vision of our life would have been heaven itself. But if they had been time-warped into our shoes — might not a good many of them have learned very soon the secrets of librium, sherry and illicit slices of bread and jam?   *Thelma Arnold*

A working wife with a career is never happy when people come to dinner because if they don't praise her cooking she feels insulted and if they do praise her cooking she feels insulted.
Terence Allingham

Being a modern wife requires so much effort. It's nice to be emancipated; but after coping with kids, cleaning, gardening and chasing the man who clears drains, it takes a stout heart to plod out in the rain to model fashions or fight a pushy bachelor in the sales office. At least our unemancipated forbears were permitted to sit and soak their feet and read a nice long novel.   *Pamela Brown*

Today's wife is often desperately undecided as to whether she should try to be (or at least seem to be in others' minds) more of a contented cow, or a discontented genius.

A. Bula

Most wives vaguely accept after years of washing up and apple pies, that their brains have simply grown old and tired and comatose. Then they get talked into a W.E.A. course. For a quarter of an hour (awkward and out of place) they listen to these strange voices apparently talking Hindi. Then a word or two begins to clarify. And suddenly they hear their own voice commenting; not the voice of Mrs B. debating the weekend meal, but the voice of Miss A. whom they'd half forgotten ever existed. It's a strange feeling – almost physical. The rust comes off the intelligence in great red flakes, the wheels mesh – and begin to grind. Nothing so painful or exacting has happened since the last baby.

Square middle-aged ladies, looking slightly drunk lurch out of dusty reading rooms clutching copies of *Othello*. The High Street seems totally different. And in bed that night their dearly loved husbands say, 'What is the matter with you – you keep moving.' And do not know that their lumpy, loving wives are mustering their arguments for this week's essay.   *Penelope Smith*

Wife's lib

My wife's the lacky who stays at home, does all the washing, cooking and yells 'I'm damn well fed up, I'm getting a job, I don't get wages for staying at home, you're out all day, travelling about meeting the women and flirting about, what about me, I want a change, stuck in the house, its like a cage.' Well, poor ole girl she's right I suppose.

M. Concannon

A wife is a MUG! What else can she be, taking on the superhuman job that she does. Ask any bloke to do the same and what would he say? 'What do you take me for, a mug or something?'
She takes a chap on, her eyes shining. And what does she get? A lifetime's work, impossible tasks, and in many cases, a life of drudgery.
I sometimes wonder how they feel when the gilt is wearing a bit thin and they are faced with a pile of dirty washing, horrible socks etc. And where could hubby be then? In the pub? On the golf course? At a soccer match? Oh, ladies, you astound me.
Occasionally he arrives home in an expansive mood expecting her to kiss him lovingly and him still smelling of the ploughman's lunch he had at midday – stale beer and onions. Ugh! *Alf Valentine*

The plethora of women's magazines gives the game away. However good they are, they are aimed at a species which loves, above all else, to cook, knit, sew, and to give complete satisfaction in bed – in short, to please. Even the articles of wider interest have the look of life to creatures trapped underground.
The men have their specialist magazines – woodworking and photography, aircraft and D.I.Y. But, then, so do women. But no one lumps men together in a magazine called Him or Father. *G. Fry*

My ma-in-law was a good wife – gentle, kind, patient, sweet-natured. My pa-in-law was a pig. For forty years he bossed her, nagged her, corrected her – until one day she ran away to senility and after a little while, died. He was furious. He went about the house in a rage of indignation.
How could you *do* this to me, Annie? How could you leave me on my own?
I do so hope the angels have got her hidden away in some quiet, happy corner of heaven, where he can never find her. *Anonymous*

At some time all wives go through an identity crisis. They are their husbands' wives, their children's mothers, the owner of Sparky the dog or the lady who always takes three pints and a yoghurt. The moment they feel a blurring of outline they should at once do a parachute jump – apply for a place in the Open University, learn the flute or organise an expedition to the Congo. Or leave a note, 'Dinner in oven. Back before morning'. And let them wonder.

Pamela Brown

A seventeenth century scold's bridle

A lot of men regard their wives as cars – not only useful, but expressing something of their husband's personality. From there it's very easy to take the next step – to trade the unfortunate woman in when smarter, newer models come on the market.

It's difficult for the newly divorced wife to get rid of the delusion that she has a placard round her neck. 'Reliable. Sound. One previous owner.'
Mary Knight

It is not her sex that keeps a woman from great achievement. A wife could never have painted the Mona Lisa: just as she got to the tricky bit of the smile, someone would have yelled upstairs for a clean shirt.
Roland Ellis

A wife holds a responsible job, pays half the bills, including the mortgage — and <u>still</u> the Inland Revenue corresponds via the husband!

E. M. Milne

Trouble and strife

A wife is your favourite pain in the neck. *Dudley Vaillant*

A wife is like Big Ben . . . constantly reminding you that it is there, and never wrong. *P. Pardy*

First Man: My wife and I have been married for forty five years and have never had a row.
Second Man: How is that? Do you live apart? *C. Nash*

A wife is someone who can say after a cutting remark, as mine did, 'If I hadn't said it, I couldn't have apologised'. *R. J. Brierley*

What is a wife?
A name for a warden of a dog-house! *A. R. Morris*

A wife is someone who whispers soft to get something. But shouts loud when she don't. *L. Jones*

A wife is a medley of moods as unpredictable as summer weather; when she's happy she will sing like a lark, when she's sad life itself seems in mourning, but exactly what turns her this way or that you will never understand. *J. Seaman*

The bad wife I would describe as a bitter half that drives her man to drink many a bitter half. *Fred Markham*

A wife can sound a real sourpuss sometimes, enough to make you wonder why her husband puts up with her. Until you meet her husband. *T. Sharot*

Just when you think you know your wife for certain, know all her faults and virtues – take care, sonny boy, your troubles have only just begun. *Jack Carter*

A wife is behind you when you're pushed. *B. Sanderson*

She's a contrary sort of creature who tells you she'd love to eat out for a change, then throws the crockery at you when you suggest moving the dining room table into the garden. *J. Oriel*

A wife is the one who gets her way, or God help you. *Alan Connor*

A wife is someone who makes a man wonder what he used to do for aggravation.

A. Ratcliffe

HORRORS!

What is a wife? It's difficult to realise mine is the beautiful little bint I married many years ago. My Ginger Rogers, Barbara Stanwyck and Marilyn Monroe all rolled into one. I thought then love was wonderful – instead of a kind of bug that can attack men of all ages.

Love, once it gets a foothold you've had it. Actually it's much more serious than chicken pox, adenoids, or what have you and longer lasting.

It was nearly a week after the fateful plunge when we had our first tiff, it's still not over. If I make a mistake it's 'You clumsy clot!' If she makes the same, it's 'Now look what you've made me do!'

A tip, don't ever pry into her affairs, well not much. Once you have found out how much the old rattlesnake has salted away, let things drop, remember Monica could be sitting pretty sooner than you expect. Bye. Bye's. *W.F.L.*

Natural history studies prove that every living creature is preyed upon by others. Some parasites, once having gained admission, change beyond all recognition to carry out their true object of destruction, or hanger-on-ism, nourishing themselves at the expense of their victim.

Man has a high quota of creatures parasitic upon him; building societies, insurance companies, income taxes and the most dangerous of all – wives.

Few men escape becoming wife-infested. This creature, once having attached herself to her prey, gradually changes her slender form, swelling and growing by absorbing the juices from the wallet. This produces weakness in the man, heightened by the increasing drain upon him when the wife parasite reproduces in kind.

Even after the host's death, this creature continues to be nourished from stored-up juice resources called savings.

Ironic, but in many cases, man is ignorant of his danger until the wife has taken up permanent quarters and begun the process of his degeneration. There is no cure – only prevention. *M. F.*

A wife is someone who was so lovely when you first got married, you could have eaten her. After a few years, you wish you had done.

B. L.

Must you clean your shoes in the kitchen?
Do you call this cup washed?
What do you do in the bathroom all this time?
Must you have two overcoats hanging in the hall wardrobe?
I've got to go shopping. You'd better get the car out.
I haven't decided where; I'll tell you when we get there.
Where's my bag? Where are my gloves?
Where's my watch? I'll tell you when I am ready.
Why are we going this way?
Is your hearing-aid switched on?
Everybody is leaving the district except us.
Do you care what you are doing to my nerves?
Why do you drive so far away from the kerb?
You're in the middle of the road; no one can pass you.
Mind. Be careful. What are you doing?
Did you see that lorry?
He's hooting at you. Did you hear what he said?
Why are you slowing down?
Why are you going so fast?
Stop here! Now, I've got to walk back.
Go further on; I've changed my mind.
Let me out here. You're holding everybody up.
Turn right.
Where are you going; you know I meant turn left.
I'll go by bus next time.
Don't shout. I'm not going to say another word.
Everybody is hooting at you. You shouldn't be allowed to drive.
Take me home. I can't stand any more.
Stop at the stationer's, I want to get you a wedding
anniversary card.   *J.S.*

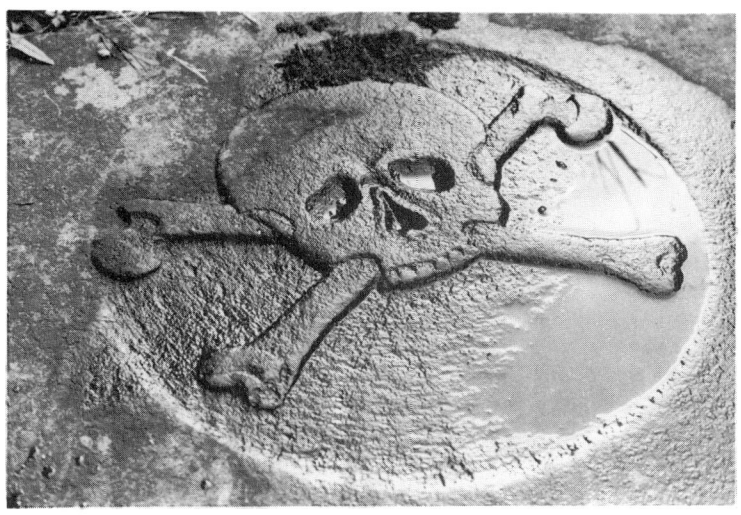

Does your husband blame you for all that goes wrong? Don't be surprised and don't expect too much chivalry. Remember the first gentleman in paradise?
'Oh, God, I am not guilty, it was Eve who seduced me.'

Zofia Lloyd

44

War of the sexes

I'm very tolerant. If I hear her drop a dozen plates on the floor I don't take any notice. Otherwise you get ulcers.

You should treat a wife the same way as the children – say yes to everything. It keeps them happy and saves a lot of arguments. The next day they'll have forgotten what they asked for and want something else.   *J.L.*

A wife is someone whose answer to, 'What have I done wrong now?', is, 'If you don't know, then I'm not going to tell you.'

The time it takes to find the answer is directly proportional to the time it took to notice that she was sulking.   *D.M.*

A wife is the one, who, after those inevitable little marital differences, thinks things out logically, and always does the forgiving. If it has been his fault, she forgives him, out of the goodness of her heart, and this makes her feel noble. If it has been her fault, she forgives him, out of the goodness of her heart, and this makes her feel doubly noble.

After all – if it hadn't been for him, it wouldn't have been her fault in the first place!   *E. A. Stewart*

A wife is one who gladly shares your bed, but claims her half in the middle!   *William Tallon*

A wife is the only woman who's always right about you being wrong.
                                                                               N. V. Ettenfield

Often as I lay beside my wife in the early morning, listening to the dawn chorus heralding the start of day and feeling the warmth of her body as she presses herself against me, her golden hair wisp-like on my shoulder, a thought pains me – 'Which one of us will go first?' But, she always gets to the bathroom before me.   *David J. Williams*

We both think alike, but she thinks first.   *E. Smith*

A wife is someone who, when you're late for the second time from the match, leaves a note saying: 'Your dinner is in the dog.'   *J. Gaff*

A wife will only have the last word if she thinks it is to her advantage!   *Edward John Gliddon*

A wife is someone who always has the first word, the middle word and the last word.   *Helene Kirkman*

*A wife can match those giant
prehistoric dinosaurs in size.
Tongue size.*

D. W. S

Nags

A wife is like a bulging purse – very handy to have around but difficult to shut up.

Pat Pardy

Wives nag. This, translated from the male argot, means they ask reasonable things reasonably. Several times. Gradually the urgency increases and the voice rises. At which point the husband tells his mates and the children tell their cronies that she's at it again. In several thousand years of evolution it has never occurred to them that if they did it the first time they'd have a purring wife and mother on their hands. And quite probably apple pie instead of a packeted whip for pudding.

Pamela Brown

When a husband gets no reply to a request he shouts a second time. When a wife gets no reply she repeats it without shouting. This is called nagging.

Angela Lansbury

A wife is someone whose utterance of flattery is called good sense, and whose utterance of good sense is called nagging.

Isabel Nuttall

I love my old moaner.

R.B.

48

She's a donkey driver

A wife is the girl for whom he would climb the highest mountain, swim the deepest ocean, brave the thickest jungle, trudge the longest highway . . .
He never swore he would clean the highest window, scour the deepest saucepan, clear the thickest brambles, tramp the longest High Street.   *F. Walker*

A wife is a person who says that before you can sow a row of peas you have to tidy the shed so that you can get at the fertilizer and the seed peas themselves. Then you have to put fresh cord on the line to make sure the row will be straight. Next you have to mow the grass on the path leading to the vegetable patch and then cut the edges of the path to make it neat and tidy. After the tools have been put away you have to tidy up the shed again and sweep up all the earth on the paths and floors and clean off your Wellingtons. It is then that you realise that you have forgotten to sow the peas.   *W. J. Nott*

Wives are the people who suddenly put up kitchen shelving after waiting for their husbands to do it for two years. Husbands are the people who come home from work and say, 'Good grief, couldn't it wait?'   *T. Forbes*

There are two words my wife loathes – tomorrow and later. So I'm learning to make up some more complicated excuses.   *Keith Nolan*

I only ever really *hated* my husband when he'd wake me to tell me the baby had poo'd.   *Joanne Wates*

A wife is the one who is full of simple home improvements that any fool can do. I am the fool who is simple enough to do them.   *D. Pyatt*

As time has passed by she's been good I'll admit.
Her words for *my darling* are now *lazy twit*.   *Doug Hamilton*

A wife looks at the things around the house that need repairing and knows why industry sometimes comes to a standstill.

Brenda Freeman

In two (or more) minds ...

A wife is the better half, with nothing to wear, who wears out a pair of shoes looking for another new pair and finally, after checking on twenty shops buys the first pair she liked at the first shop.

J. E. Robson

A wife is someone who reads horror books in bed and then wakes you up and tells you to turn the light out because she is frightened stiff.

John Brady

When I am half-way through decorating one room, only a wife could tell me she is thinking about what colours she will have in another.

John Edwards

She calls me to remove a spider ... Then just when I've swatted it asks me to promise not to kill it.

Trevor Sharot

A wife is someone who gives you two ties for your birthday, and when you wear one, she asks you why you don't like the other.

P. Regan

A wife is someone who scrubs and polishes when expecting visitors then apologizes for the mess.

E. Atkinson

A wife says, 'You never take me out', and when I say, 'Let's go', has nothing to wear.

P. Mills

A wife will tell you how fat you are getting and then will burst into tears because you refuse to eat her freshly baked chocolate sponge pudding.

B. G. Edwards

My wife insists on a room being decorated when it's quite unnecessary. Then when it's finished she decides she liked it better as it was.

Frederick Tinker

She is someone who bursts into tears when he forgets an anniversary, and equally bursts into tears when he buys her some roses.

Elizabeth Gozney

A wife is someone who insists that she looks a sight but gets upset if you agree.

E. A.

My wife complained about my continually leaving the cap off the toothpaste, so I resolved to make amends. After a week she eyed me suspiciously, saying 'Why aren't you brushing your teeth these days?'
G. W. Sanders

A wife is someone who will clean the house from top to bottom before the cleaning woman comes.
S. Reynolds

A wife is a woman who says, 'Of course I don't mind you going to the office party tonight!' Then when you rush back home nice and early before 10.00 pm she storms, 'And where the hell have you been?'.
Cecil G. Curran

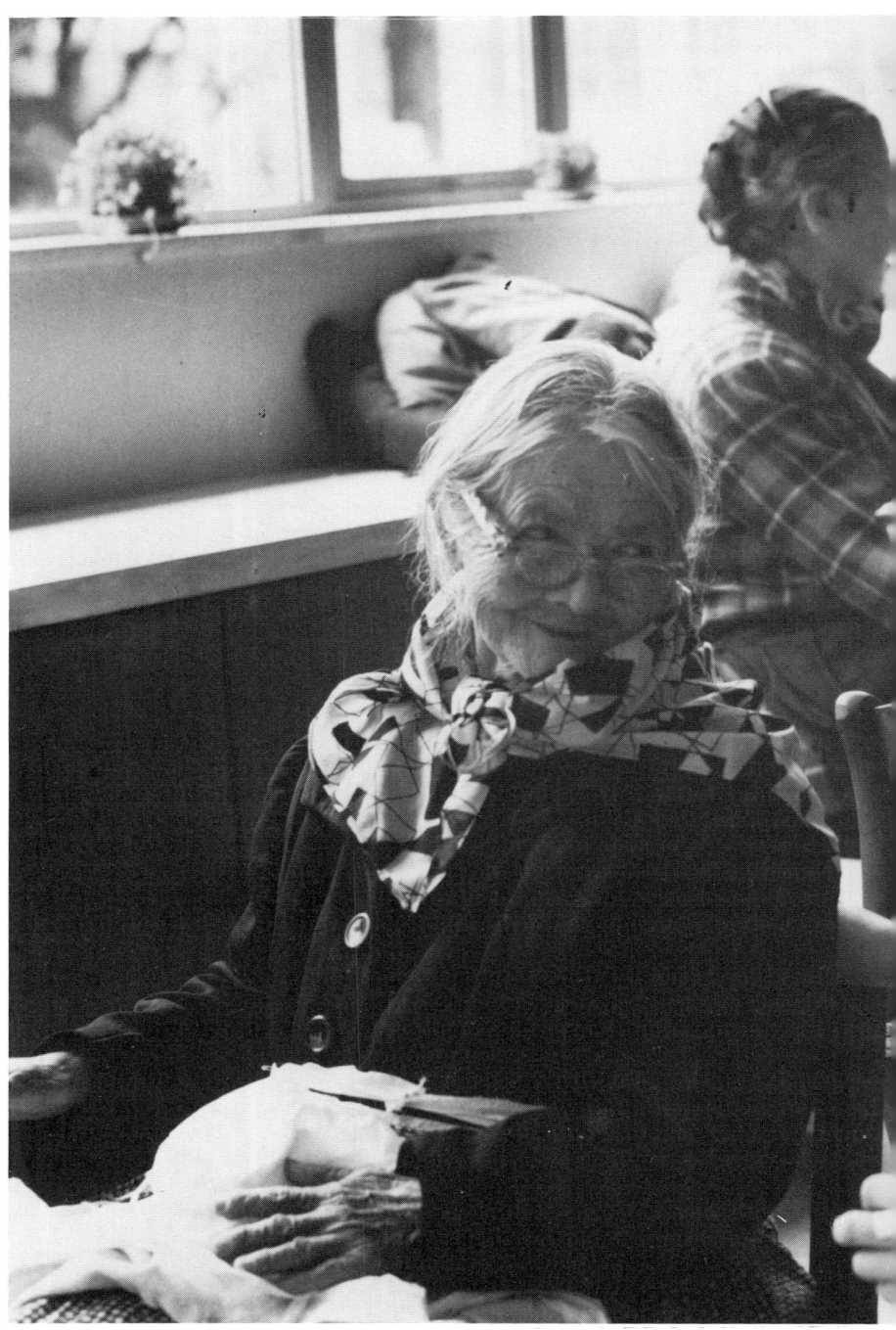

Forever young

She's grown old so very imperceptibly. She loves to remember our early days, our Springtime. She talks about them, not from mere nostalgia – more from pride. These are the things we did together, the plans we made, and now she can smile at the mistakes we made, and now, how our pictures of the future, in fact actually turned out. She's the power that keeps our family – no longer with us – always together in spirit – the grandchildren always eager to visit. The quiet, efficient power that keeps the diary safely covered for the weeks ahead; who knows my moods and waits patiently for me to climb out of them. The supreme listener on whom I can unload my worries, my bright ideas. One who'll be able to sit, just sit, while anger melts and tensions fade away. The good companion with whom I can walk happily to the end of the road.   *F. G. Hollis*

Let's go back some forty odd years. Who was this girl with brown eyes, who from first meeting captured me, led me in a daze to the altar, mothered me and our children through the years, put up with me. Now as the years become clouded with perhaps sadness and pain, and fear of the future, who is this who still stands beside me, making the ties that hold us even more binding? Needing my support and comfort more now. God forbid that I should, as long as I have breath, ever forsake or let down, this life's companion – my wife.   *A. L. Fry*

A wife is someone who is 'beautiful' in her husband's eyes after forty two years of marriage. When my husband was asked by a young bank receptionist if she could help him, he said he was looking for his wife. 'What is she like?' 'She has a blue dress and is very beautiful', he replied. I wonder what she thought when we both went in a little later!   *H. Sellers*

I'd choose her again anytime, anywhere. Put her in a crowd of beautiful, intelligent girls and I'd choose her. That's because she's good for me and her tum doesn't put my middle-age spread to shame.

Dave Mason

53

A quiet strength

A wife walks slower, feels softer, cries more often. But she's the strength behind our family. *Benny Lloyd*

A wife is someone who calls you the worst names she can think of, but should anyone else do the same, turns on them like a tiger defending her young. *J. Mansell*

A wife is someone who will mow the lawns, but do it on a weekday so that you can't watch her and feel guilty. *M. Richards*

After a night out with the boys, when you return (slightly inebriated), who is waiting to bawl you out – your wife, God bless her. *R. J. Gibbons*

A wife is someone who does more for you than your hands, supports you better than your legs, complains less than your stomach, understands you better than your brain and stays with you longer than your hair. *A. Ratcliffe*

Men, when they are made redundant, or retire, or fail in some enterprise are often almost overwhelmed. The world goes on without them and they are aghast.
Wives learn in little ways. Their work is undone every day – food eaten, brightness dulled. And their capacity for renewal unnoticed. For twenty years their energies are centred on their children – and yet, all the time they know they care for them only to release them. Even in joy they remain wary. They know the circling of days. *Mark Hewitt*

What is a wife? She is Gran to twelve grandchildren. Through our thirty-six years together we have known gladness and pain and hardship, but always she says, 'never mind, love, it will work out'. When she went into hospital for an op and I went in to see her, speech failed me as I saw her looking so pale. Our hands met, 'Don't worry love, everything's all right' she said. I turned my head so that she wouldn't see the tears. What is a wife? Simply, she's my life. *W. J. Price*

A wife is a partner whose unspoken words could be 'What can I give to marriage to bring lasting happiness to us both?'

John A. Calderon

Love is forever

I suppose one doesn't discover what being a wife is until the end of one's life. When one is young it's the adventures that matter, the surprises, the successes, the red-letter days. But now I see even my wedding day as nothing at all set against the learning years of love, the years he and I have had together. Just as the recollection of the birth of my children is an anecdote beside the story of their growing and maturity.

Now I am old I look at all I've done in my life and the great excitements, the times when my stomach knotted and my blood raced, are like tales told of someone else. It's the slow, steady times that are part of me, relationships, and achievements built little by little, so quietly they scarcely seemed to grow at all. Those times of passion and adventure when I was young seem like fairy gold that have turned to dead leaves – whereas the long ordinariness of my marriage shines untarnished. *Moira Hamilton*

A wife is the one who tends you with love and gentleness when health breaks down, who dishes up the little favourite snacks when appetite has fled, who bathes your feet and trims your nails when you are no longer able to bend. *D. Williams*

When she consented to dance, the first time I met her, I held her hand.
In cinemas, on country walks I held her hand.
When promising to honour and cherish, I held her hand.
When each child was born I held her hand.
Such small hands! Golden hands! Amazingly creative – to economise. Hard worked and roughened they may have been, but only smoothness was sensed in her caressing.
Now the hands are blue-veined, drawn white but still active. Cool on my fevered head, warm and comforting when I am down. And if we go to church or shop, in fact anywhere I always hold that precious hand. *George Somerville*

My wife sings in the morning, just looks at me with twinkling blue eyes. She prayed for me whilst I was in Battle of the Somme, I felt a protection over there. We married when we were teenagers and she always backed me in my despair. A very lovable lady now of eighty one years. I challenge anyone to find a better one.
William C. Martin

She is the greatest! The tomboy I kicked the ball around with seventy years ago. The lovely bride who walked down the aisle with me fifty years ago. Wait – that's not all – she gave me seven wonderful kids, nursed me through six major operations and worked till she was sixty four in spite of ill health.
This 11th April is our 'Golden Day'.
Sorry Mohammed Ali you ain't the greatest! *Percy Neeves*

56

What is a wife? What a daft question. She is, or at least mine is, a complete DIY kit, the best ever made by God. We've hit up nearly fifty years between us, and we both love one another dearly. I still have only got to look across a crowded room and I can see her at once. At night as she lays in her bed beside mine I slip my hand in hers and take her down memory lane with me, way back, back to the cliffs in Kent where we did our courting, up to the ward where I waited for our first baby, nearly hating it for what it was doing to her. Good times, lots of bad times, always with love and trust. The last war, never doubting her love and affection during our precious leaves. A few more babies. Then my illness, her love never faltered. Dirty washing, a sixty year old baby. It was her that made me battle on. Three months, the doctor said. Well, she said, let's have a good three months. That was nearly nine years ago. I'm on my legs, just. I use a wheel chair but there's less for her to do. Now I can do very little but I can eat by myself and toilet myself again. And still we hold hands, and as I say, dream and wander back through the past and look forward to the future, what there is of it. For me, a wife? God's most precious gift and my most beloved friend and companion.

Joseph Barber

I love every hair on her snow-white head.

Kenneth McBride

57

Without her

Without her laughter a room full of babbling people feels cold and empty.

N. Naidoo

Without Judy I'd suddenly feel forty-one years, two months and eleven days old, after all.

Robert North

They all think I'm tough, successful even macho. Only she knows. I'm weak, I'm like a lost puppy without her.

Hugh Cottrell

Without a wife husbands would all look like Norman Wisdom.

P. Gilchrist

A wife, good or bad, is a man's reason for living, for working and for trying. Without her, old age would be a terrifying thought.
A bad wife needs a good husband to help her. A bad husband needs a good wife to help him.

Lilian Oxley

Now that she's gone

The saddest paradox of all is that the more deeply we love, the more deeply we must sorrow. It seems a heavy price to pay – but I look at those unfortunates who have never loved and they seem shadows. When I lost my wife I thought I had lost half my life – but I found after a while she had left me a bequest – herself. She is closer now than she ever was.   *John Hogan*

I know my husband would have liked me to send these few lines. We scribbled them together, before he passed away this Christmas:
Spring, Summer, Autumn, Winter
All these seasons, she never alters.
As I look back, I bless that Spring day
That has lasted until my Winter day
But alas I know I have to go
And leave my Spring lass
Whom I love so.   *M. K. Smith*

What is a wife? There can only be one answer – my world, for she was my whole world. Whatever I now have, I owe to my dear wife. Without her, life has become a mere empty existence. My only solace is to visit the sacred plot where my dear one rests and murmur a few words of affection. All else is grief.   *Charles Mutch*

Dearest one,
An entry against April 24th in my new diary reads: 'Indebted to J.W. for constancy, loyalty, confidence, home-building, native ability, humility, inspiration and enduring love. For anything I can do I am indebted to her'. Dates mean much to me, and on November 9th I will again see the open book at the crematorium.
I marvel at your patience with difficult me for our forty-three years. I'm a concertinist and practised most days, perhaps twelve thousand. Most boring at times, but I cannot recall a word of complaint.
A true home-builder. How I miss your beautifully thought out meals and the touch of femininity about Beechleaf Cottage and garden which you so loved. You taught our boys by practice and precept the value of honesty.
Always you were so reliable. The only promise you ever broke was to leave me so suddenly and unexpectedly some $3\frac{1}{4}$ years ago, when in hospital overnight, and I was not there with you. For, remember you sometimes said, discussing the future 'Don't worry, I won't leave you . . .'
But maybe I'm wrong, and you didn't leave us. You kept your promise. Your sweet influence and spiritual presence are near, helping me to carry on.

Yours only, Bram
W. Bramwell Thornett

Your wife is your home – your life – in fact everything – she is the dreadful loss you have to bear if you have to part. You'll remember everything and it won't mean anything to anybody but you two. You will never forget it – but it's something to treasure and thank God for – and especially to help you live without her.   *J. Bell*

When he is ill she will nurse him and when he is dying, she will fetch him from the hospital, so he may die in his own familiar surroundings.
Her final act of love will be to wash his dear dead body and to be thankful that he was not now in pain.

Winifred S. David,
widow of Dave

I was a wife for forty-five years. I wish I had loved more, considered more, and listened instead of nagged, but that's life.   *G. O. Matthews*

The long view

What is a wife? Perhaps the answer has, through all history, been another question: 'What does a man require of a woman in payment for his protection?' Against tiger, Saxon, menial job or the tight, smug smiles of safely married women?

And surely now question and answer fail, for any woman in the Western world is free to escape from dreariness or the confines of a parental home into a more fulfilling world and to live safe and secure and happily occupied without the strong right arm of any man about her. She can explore her sexuality without any legal licence. Surely now if she chooses to marry it will be for wider, kinder reasons than when the wolves were snapping at her heels? Today a woman can decide whether to have children or whether to keep her job once she is married. She can live in two worlds simultaneously, unlike her ancestors. She is redefining the word 'wife'.

The demarcation wall between the roles of husband and wife is down, or crumbling. A husband – with a little luck – will see that there is no loss of face in pushing a pram, changing a nappy or choosing tomatoes with his baby slung about his neck in its sling. If he gets home first he is capable of turning on the oven, putting on the kettle, drawing the curtains against the evening's cold.

And she, the wife, knows a spark plug from a banana and can change a fuse with only the minimum of trepidation.

In theory. For several thousand years have left their patterning on the human heart. Love, that lure set by nature to ensure the survival of the species, sends us temporarily mad. Emancipation is forgotten – or can be manipulated by the least blinded of the partners – and the golden age of equality and reason gets put off for another millennium.

The new style wife with the ring upon her emancipated finger, her baby snug in its Babygro, the washing chuntering quietly in the automatic, looks about her mortgaged home and, a little guiltily, wonders. For it isn't working out quite as she had planned.

She finds she can keep up her old job – teaching or typing, calculating or cooking – still retain her old personality and abilities, even though she has lost her name and changed her status; plan her family as efficiently as an office schedule – but her love, her dear, her equal and her friend can still turn medieval if his dinner is delayed. The car seems to be his, rather than a family possession. And babies are Neanderthal in their life style.

She may be her employer's paragon, but at home she frequently finds herself having to bite her tongue as she is scolded, usually amiably enough, for some small incompetence. She finds herself apologising rather too much. Determined to be a patient, reasonable wife and a civilized human being she stifles her cave dwelling instincts – and has taken the first step to doormat. Of course, if she does throw the plate she has taken the first step towards being labelled shrew. Either of these roles can be used at some later date to drive the husband to drink, rugby football or a younger woman. And the agony aunts will tell her it was *entirely* her fault.

As it is, they will chide her constantly, as they did in the days of Victoria. He, the breadwinner, is still permitted to sag, to snore, to gloom. She must not. Not only must she be bright and attractive, sweet smelling (no word about his over-powering 'manliness'), attentive, a bolsterer of egos, a listener to woes, but in the more intelligent and progressive magazines she may find herself being rapped severely over the knuckles for objecting to his unfaithfulness or his sexual aberrations. She is not permitted headaches, colds, temper, bad backs, boredom or absent-mindedness.

After a day when the baby and the cat have been sick, the shopping was done in a series of snow flurries, the milk did not come and the soup burned dry while she was endeavouring to be polite to two Seventh Day Adventists, topped by her husband sleeping all evening with his mouth open, she must be prepared to flare to ardour at his touch. If, on the other hand, she turns to him hopefully, she may well be met with the alarm engendered by a raving nymphomaniac. She has the manufacturers' assistance in her attempts to live the good life . . . but if she fails and her goulash comes out of a packet, she will not be allowed to feel comfortable about it. The lady experts will frown and point grimly to the stockpot. For to be an ideal wife she must be what she was – well-groomed, well-dressed, efficient, amusing and informed – though on a fraction of her former income and barred from all male companionship save on the most shallow of footings (watch the eyes of a best friend narrow as one begins to enjoy a conversation with her husband) – and at the same time be adept at every housewifely skill. Though, it must be said, her old attractions and abilities must now be fitted with a thermostat. She may shine – but never, *never* more brightly than her husband. This, say the columnists, damages his personality and can lead to almost anything.

The label of Good Plain Cook is no accolade: even the humblest woman's magazine demands a good working knowledge of patisserie and wine, papillotes and terrine. Plain knitting is no longer enough. The wool shops are a jungle of strange and exotic skeins and the ladies breathe heavily down their noses if asked for a nice, simple, plain pattern. Woks squat on the shelves of every cookery department and vegetables grow unrecognisable.

The wife who cannot add a degree or a diploma, an art or a craft, a civic, church or charitable offering to her normal duties of lawyer, seamstress, cleaner, cook, nurse and chauffeur, clerk and vet, electrician, plumber, gardener, glazier, carpenter, sewer-man and rat-catcher is not worth her salt.

The ad men cajole and bully. The psychologists tell her that she is pushing her child too hard, her husband too hard – and that she is not becoming involved enough in their progress. When she finally feels justifiably guilty they tell her she's stressed and put her on to Librium. She cannot even retire to bed in a long white nightdress, as her grandmother did, and love in the secret dark. There are manuals. She feels an entirely new wave of guilt for not wanting to make love on the back lawn by moonlight.

Mum and Aunt Maud live two hundred miles away so she can no longer run away from home for the afternoon. The corner shop with the bentwood chair and the nice round lady with a sweetie for the baby is gone. The new wife must gird her loins and safari off through the inhuman scaling of the local hypermarket, threatened on every side by cascades of lavatory rolls and walls of after-dinner mints and driven to a dazed insanity by a selection from Strauss.

She attempts to remember her budget and ignore the goodies that in mother's day were safely shut into Fortnum's. She also tries to ignore cheap offers, competition lures, catalogues and book club bait. The media says she can have everything she wants. She evolves a sort of monitor to block their siren voices – and tries to plug the ears of her children against them too.

She becomes a compulsive picker-upper. She tries to remember to clear out pockets before she does the wash. She takes on the role of General Demon when she sets times to be home, asks about homework, says 'No' to four-inch heels for her twelve year old. She takes the cat to the vet. And buries it. She makes people take back families of mice they have been given. She takes in a new cat. She moves house. She entertains his boss.

She is called 'Mum' by the greengrocer. People at the door ask if her husband is in. Her television programmes are switched over. Her Mozart is given odd overtones by the heavy rock that is finding its own level through the ceiling. Sometimes she feels very, very sorry for herself.

And it is then that the miracles happen. She goes out to the car and finds he's cleaned the frost off the windows. Her teenage son gives her a split bag of pork scratchings. And cleans out the garage. The cat hooks his thin, velvet legs around her neck and declares his undying devotion. Lifelines.

And if she's very lucky and by some trick of fate has found a husband with sense and kindliness, one day he will put his arm about her shoulders and say 'To hell with the specialists. To hell with the books on how to improve your sex life, how to raise your kids, how to change your hair, your dining room, your rockery, your I.Q. You are the person I want. I'll back you if you've got urges to practise transcendental meditation or pottery, batik or Medieval Latin, ladies' football or long-distance running. For I love you, not this nameless, formless 'wife' they talk about.

'We've both made hundreds of mistakes, some so awful it's hard even to think about them, and will make plenty more before we're through. We're no more perfect than the last hundred generations have been. But we're not too bad, you know. And when the kids have taken their egos and their demands further afield, there will be some good times still for you and me.'

And that is when she finds that, after all, she's glad she's someone's wife. On the whole. Of course, being a man he may never get round to saying it – and she may never know.

Not for *sure*.

Pamela Brown

64